MW01154747

HANDS-ON GEOLOGY

Get Hands-On with

Erosion!

Alix Wood

Full of real geology experiments that help you learn all about erosion.

PowerKiDS press

New York

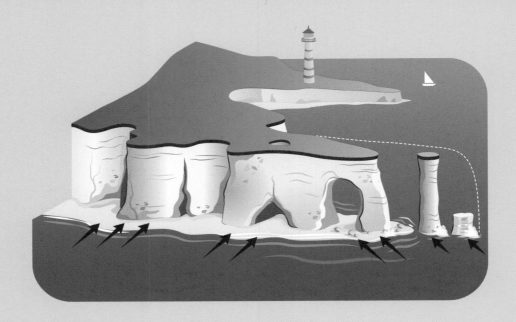

Published in 2022 by Rosen Publishing
29 East 21st Street, New York, NY 10010

Copyright © 2021 Alix Wood Books

Adaptations to North American edition © 2021
by Rosen Publishing

Produced for Rosen Publishing by Alix Wood Books
Designed by Alix Wood
Editor: Eloise Macgregor
Consultant: Kate Spencer, Professor of Environmental Geochemistry

Cataloging-in-Publication Data
Names: Wood, Alix.
Title: Get hands-on with erosion! / Alix Wood.
Description: New York : PowerKids Press, 2022. | Series: Hands-on geology | Includes glossary and index.
Identifiers: ISBN 9781725331198 (pbk.) | ISBN 9781725331211 (library bound) |
ISBN 9781725331204 (6 pack) | ISBN 9781725331228 (ebook)
Subjects: LCSH: Erosion--Juvenile literature.
Classification: LCC QE571.W66 2022 | DDC 551.3'02--dc23

Photo credits:
2, 4 top, 6, 8, 9, 10 top, 11 top, 12, 14 top, 15 top, 18 bottom, 19 top, 20 bottom, 22 top, 24 top and
bottom, 28 top, 29 top © AdobeStock Images;
all other illustrations @ Alix Wood

Printed in the United States of America
CPSIA Compliance Information: Batch #CSPK22. For Further Information contact Rosen Publishing, New York, New York at 1-800-237-9932.

Contents

What Is Erosion?

Erosion is when natural forces such as water, wind, ice, and **gravity** transport worn rocks and soil from one place to another. This process is part of the rock cycle. Before material can be eroded, it needs to be weathered—broken down so it is small enough to be carried away. While strong stream currents might be able to move a boulder, a light breeze can only transport tiny fragments.

What forces do you think wore away this coast road?

The Rock Cycle

Once rock is weathered, the pieces get washed or blown away, often into rivers or the oceans. The pieces settle and form a layer known as **sediment**. This sediment gets pressed and compacted and sinks underground.

There, the sediment is heated and pressed into new rock, or melted by the high temperatures under Earth's surface to form a liquid rock known as **magma**.

Forces underground lift the newly formed rock to the surface. In this way, all the **minerals** that make up Earth's rocks are constantly recycled!

Think About This... ❓
Can you find the three main types of rock in this diagram?

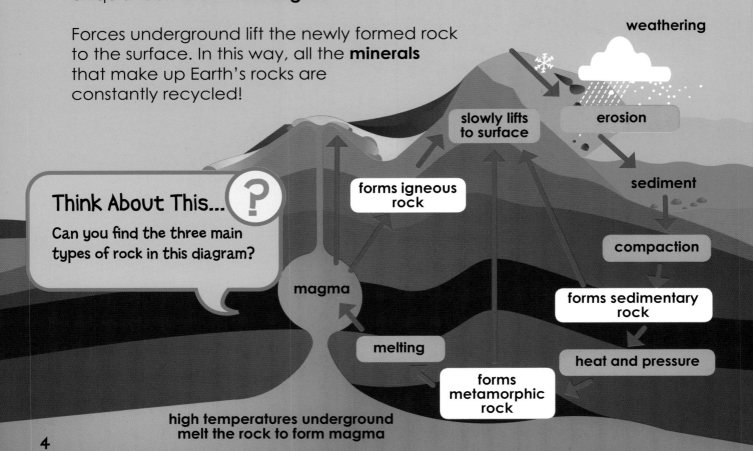

weathering

slowly lifts to surface

erosion

forms igneous rock

sediment

compaction

magma

forms sedimentary rock

melting

heat and pressure

forms metamorphic rock

high temperatures underground melt the rock to form magma

Weathering, Erosion, Deposition—What's the Difference?

Weathering is the process of breaking down rock and soil. If rock is broken down, but stays where it is, the process is called weathering.

Erosion is the process of carrying rock and soil away. Weathering helps erosion by breaking rock into small, easy-to-carry pieces.

Deposition drops sediment in a new place. A river might move sediment downstream and then drop it (deposit it) there.

Weathering

BREAKS IT

Erosion

MOVES IT

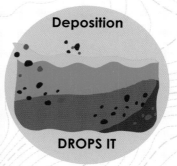

Deposition

DROPS IT

The ocean can weather and erode rock at the same time! Waves crash into the rock and break it into smaller pieces, and then carry those pieces out to sea.

HANDS-ON Break It, Move It, Drop It

You will need:
- a small bowl
- some pebbles
- some damp soil
- a flat dish
- a thin book
- a jug of water

Fill a bowl with a mixture of damp soil and pebbles. Tap the bowl to move the soil into all the gaps. Place a flat dish on top of the bowl. Holding the bowl and the dish, turn them both over. Lift the bowl, and your pebble mountain should now be on the dish.

Prop one end of the dish on a book, to form a slope. Slowly pour water on your mountain. You should see the water begin to BREAK up the soil. The river the water creates will MOVE the soil down the slope, and then DROP the soil at the bottom of the slope.

Breaking Up Rocks by Weathering

For material to be small enough to be carried by wind or water, it has to be broken into pieces. This process is known as weathering, because it is weather—the water and the temperature—that breaks the rock.

Types of Weathering

Rock is broken by **physical**, **chemical**, and **biological weathering**. Sometimes separately, but usually together, these processes change the structure of rock, making it softer and easily breakable.

Physical weathering

Weathering by wind, waves, water, and ice.

Water gets into cracks in rock and freezes. As water freezes, it expands, forcing the crack open and splitting the rock.

Chemical weathering

Liquids or gases making changes to the chemicals that make up a rock.

Acid rain can dissolve soft rock. The limestone in this building has been eroded by acid rain.

Biological weathering

Weathering caused by plants and animals.

Limpets weather rock in two ways. They secrete an acid and they scratch at the rock as they feed.

HANDS-ON   Find Local Weathering

You will need:
- adult help
- a notepad
- a pencil
- a camera

Ask a trusted adult to walk with you around your neighborhood to find examples of weathered rock. Good places to look are by rivers, lakes, the coast, or on windswept high ground. Look at old buildings, too. Can you find smooth rock, worn patterns, or cracking? Take photographs or make drawings of any examples that you find.

BE A GEOLOGIST
See How Ice Can Break Rocks

You Will Need:

- small balloon
- some water
- 3 cups of flour
- a bowl
- a bread board
- a freezer
- a little patience

The Geology:

You can tell water expands as it freezes by filling an ice cube tray with water. When the ice cubes have frozen they often stick out the top of the tray. When the water in your balloon freezes, it expands, just like water inside a crack in a rock would. Did your rock crack open under the pressure of the expanding ice?

How to Do the Experiment:

To make your rock, fill a balloon with water until it is around the size of a golf ball. Squeeze any air out and tie the balloon closed.

Measure the flour into a bowl. Gradually add around 1.5 cups of water. Knead the mixture until it forms a soft dough.

Roll out a tennis ball-size lump of dough a quarter of an inch (0.5 cm) thick. Place the balloon on the dough and carefully wrap the dough around it, smoothing any cracks. Leave it to dry. This may take a couple of days. Once dry, put it in the freezer overnight.

Can you predict what will happen? Take the rock out and have a look. What did the water in the balloon do?

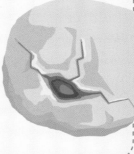

Weathering by Water and Wind

Physical weathering by wind, waves, and water change the **landscape** of our coastlines. Coastal areas tend to have strong winds, and waves pick up and throw rock as they crash onto the shore. Wind causes weathering in deserts too. Strong winds pick up particles of sand and blast the surface of rock as they whistle by. Wind also causes rocks to rub against each other, smoothing their surfaces.

Worn Smooth by Flowing Water

When rocks weather each other by rubbing together, this is known as **abrasion**. Rocks in a riverbed are worn smooth by abrasion as the **current** repeatedly knocks them into one another.

Broken Up by Salt

Waves hurl salt water into the cliff faces. Salt in seawater can force rock apart. How? Seawater gets washed into cracks and holes in the rock. In hot countries where the water **evaporates** quickly, it leaves salt **deposits** behind. The deposits build up over time and start to press outward, eventually breaking the rock.

Strong wind and seawater over the years have eroded the coast of Heping Island, Taiwan, forming these interesting-shaped rocks. The weathered sandstone contains hundreds of **fossils** too.

HANDS-ON Dissolving Rock

You will need:

- water
- some salt
- a piece of chalk
- a plate
- a teaspoon

Many minerals can be dissolved by water. Put a small pile of salt on a plate. Drop some water onto the salt using a teaspoon. What happens? Try the same experiment with a stick of chalk. Leave it in the water overnight. What happens?

BE A GEOLOGIST
Making and Weathering Mud Pies

You Will Need:

- a bucket of garden soil
- some water
- sandpaper
- eye protection
- spray bottle
- a small container
- an outside space
- a notepad and pencil
- a little patience

The Geology:

Your dried mud pies behave very much like rock would under the same circumstances, but over many years.

How to Do the Experiment:

To make your mud pies, add water to the soil until wet, but not runny. Press a handful of mud into a patty. Make around five or six, as you will use some of them later in the book. Leave them to dry for 2 to 3 days in a warm place.

Mimic weathering by windblown sand by rubbing some sandpaper over a dry mud pie. Wear eye protection, as the dust can irritate your eyes. Try rubbing at different speeds and pressures. Try different grades of paper, too. Record your results.

Try spraying a mud pie with water. Spray it from different angles, then concentrate on just one spot. Record what happens.

This one might be messy, so cover up. Place a mud pie in a container and cover it with water. Then mimic the action of waves by rocking the container back and forth. Record what happens.

Chemical Weathering

Chemical weathering is when water or gases make changes to the chemicals that make up a rock. Water can dissolve a mineral, add water to a mineral, or react with a mineral. Gases such as oxygen can alter a rock's chemistry too. For instance, oxygen caused this magnetite (right) to rust.

How does a rock rust? **Oxygen** in the air reacts with iron in some rock to form iron oxide, or rust. Iron oxide is a different color and much softer than the original rock. The reaction happens even faster if water or salt is present.

The amount of rust in an old rock can tell geologists how much oxygen was in the atmosphere long ago.

HANDS-ON Experiment with Rust

You will need:
- some fine steel wool from a paint store (dish-washing steel wool does not work as well)
- 3 glasses
- some water
- salt
- paper labels
- a notepad and pencil

Steel is a combination of iron and carbon. When iron is exposed to the air, it starts to rust. Try this experiment to watch rust in action, and see if water or salt water speeds up the reaction.

Fill two of the glasses with water. Add salt to one of them. Write labels for each glass.

Tear the steel wool into three and place a piece in each glass. Observe what happens each day in your notebook. Which wool rusted the fastest? What conditions do you think will cause rock to rust quickly?

Think About This... ❓

Adding salt to water causes **particles** to move more easily than they do in pure water. Do you think that will make the steel wool rust faster?

Water

Salt Water

Air

When **carbon dioxide**, **sulfur**, and **nitrogen** in the air react with water, they cause **acid rain**. Acid rain breaks down some types of rock, such as marble, chalk, and limestone. Acid rain helps create caves. It also creates an unusual rocky landscape called **karst**.

Karst is an area of limestone full of holes and caves. One of the most spectacular examples is the Stone Forest, near Kunming, China. The limestone has been worn away to form a landscape of hundreds of sharp, rocky towers.

Stone Forest near Kunming, China

BE A GEOLOGIST
Make Your Own Chalk Cave

You Will Need:

- large piece of natural chalk or a big stick of pavement chalk
- vinegar
- a teaspoon

The Geology:

Chalk is made of a type of limestone. Acid in the vinegar reacts with the chalk, dissolving it and producing carbon dioxide gas. The same process happens when acid in **groundwater** dissolves limestone.

How to Do the Experiment:

Scratch a small hole in the chalk using the end of the teaspoon. Then use the teaspoon to drop some vinegar into the hole. The vinegar will react with the chalk, and you should see small bubbles appear.

Once there are no more bubbles, pour away the old vinegar and add some fresh vinegar. Repeat this until your cave is the size you want.

Where do you think the chalk goes in this experiment?

Rock-Breaking Plants and Animals

Have you ever seen a sidewalk cracked by the roots of a tree? **Biological weathering** is a type of weathering caused by plants and animals.

Roots

When plants grow in holes and cracks in rock, their roots exert pressure on rock as they grow. Known as wedging, the roots eventually expand the gaps until the rock splits apart.

Fungi and Bacteria

Some biological weathering causes chemical changes. **Lichen**, fungus, and mold produce rock-eating acid. Dead roots and leaves release carbon as they rot—which, mixed with water, forms a weak acid. Some bacteria remove nitrogen from minerals in rock. This weakens the rock, making it more easily weathered by wind and water.

Animals

Some types of clams burrow into solid rock. The chemicals in animal poop and urine can also break down minerals in rock. Animals walking on rocky slopes can cause rocks to slip and scrape against each other. Burrowing animals bring rocks to the surface to be weathered by other agents.

Think About This...

Humans are a type of animal. Can you think of any ways that human activity might break up rock or cause it to weather?

BE A GEOLOGIST
Spot Some Causes of Weathering

How many causes of weathering can you see in this picture? The answers are written below.

Answers: Fox poop and rotting leaves creating acids, mole hole bringing rock to the surface, goat and people disturbing rock as they walk, tractor disturbing rocks, tree roots cracking rock, lichen growing on rocks and producing acids.

Erosion—Moving the Material

Once weathering has broken rock down, the forces of erosion take over to move the material away. Water, wind, ice, and gravity can all move rocks, stone, or sand grains away from their location. Wind may only be able to move small particles, but it can move very large amounts of small particles! For example, wind created enormous **sand dunes** in the Gobi Desert, China, that are over 1,300 feet (400 m) high!

Wind Erosion

Just as with weathering, more than one force can cause erosion in a place. Geologists believe wind erosion was one of the forces that shaped the Grand Canyon. Strong winds blow through the canyons, blowing particles into the water to be carried away.

Think About This... ❓

Can you see another force in this picture that has formed the Grand Canyon?

HANDS-ON   Make a Sand Dune

You will need:
- some newspaper
- sand
- a baking pan
- a straw

A sand dune is a hill of loose sand built by wind. They form when an obstruction stops the sand from traveling past, so it piles up. Try making a sand dune. Cover a table with newspaper. Pour sand into a baking pan. Press a rock into the sand. Hold a straw just above the sand and blow gently through it toward the rock. Remove the straw from your mouth between each breath so you don't breathe in sand. The sand will gradually form a sand dune around the rock. Experiment with different obstructions and see how your dunes change shape.

BE A GEOLOGIST
Make a Wind-Eroded Rock Formation

You Will Need:

adult help needed

- some damp sand
- a small bucket
- a hair dryer
- some flat rocks small enough to fit in the bucket
- a large cardboard box
- some thick cardboard

The Geology:

Wind can carve channels and shapes in solid stone. Different rock types weather at different rates. Granite rock weathers slowly. Limestone is easily weathered. Rocks that resist weathering remain and form ridges or hills. The surrounding, less-resistant rocks are worn away like the sand in this experiment.

How to Do the Experiment:

Design a rock formation by stacking some flat stones on top of each other. Place a handful of damp sand in the bottom of the bucket. Now rebuild your rock formation, from the top down, in the bucket. Pack damp sand around it to hold it in place as you build. Finish with a flat layer of damp sand.

This can get messy so you may want to do it outside. Put the cardboard box on its side. Place some thick cardboard over the bucket. Turn the bucket upside down and then lift it off. Put the cardboard, with the sandcastle on it, in the box.

Ask an adult to help you—anything electrical is dangerous, especially near water. Put the hair dryer on a low setting and point it at the sandcastle. You should see sand gradually eroding away as it dries and is blown to the back of the box. Increase the setting if nothing happens. Your rock formation should gradually start to appear.

Erosion—the Power of Water

Crashing waves, heavy rain, powerful waterfalls, and gushing rivers all help transport weathered rock. Water is the most common cause of erosion.

BE A GEOLOGIST
Water Erosion Experiments

You Will Need:

- a baking sheet
- some soil
- a teaspoon
- water
- some books
- a cup
- a notebook and pencil
- a spray bottle full of water
- a camera if you have one

The Geology:

Heavy rain loosens particles and transports them downhill. You will see brown water appear at the bottom of your slope, showing it is now full of eroded material.

On steep slopes, the force of gravity means water will flow faster and may cause a mudslide. A sudden large amount of water causes the soil to saturate, meaning it cannot soak up any more liquid. This is how floods happen.

How to Do the Experiment:

Form some damp soil into a slope at one end of a baking sheet. Leave the other end free of soil. To see the effect of water erosion, try these experiments. Take notes, and make drawings or photograph what happens with each experiment.

Different types of rain

Create rain by dripping water on the soil using a teaspoon. Try dripping it on the same spot, and different spots. Then spray the soil. Spray from different angles. If your spray bottle has different settings, try them out. Take notes. Look at the area at the bottom of your slope. Does water appear there? What color is it?

Water on a slope

Rebuild your soil landscape. Pour away any excess water. Put some books under the soil end of the baking sheet to create a slope. Repeat the drip and spray experiments and compare your results.

Floods

Rebuild your soil landscape. Tip a cup of water, all at once, on the soil. What happens?

Waterfalls

Waterfalls are created where areas of hard rock and soft rock meet in a riverbed. The soft rock erodes more quickly, forming a step. The force of the falling water creates a plunge pool. The overhanging ledge of the waterfall will eventually collapse, and the fallen rock erodes the pool even more. Waterfalls constantly move upriver as more and more rock erodes.

hard rock

soft rock

plunge pool

Think About This...

Why do you think earthquakes, landslides, and volcanoes might also cause waterfalls to form?

HANDS-ON Erode Your Own Waterfall

You will need:
- a dish pan
- a large pile of sand
- a small chopping board or similar
- water
- a jug

Make a large sand pile in the dish pan. The sand represents the soft rock layer. Push the board into one side of the sand pile, about halfway up, angled down a little. The board represents the hard rock layer.

Pour water onto the same side of the sand pile that you pushed the board into. Watch what happens.

The water will flow down the sandy slope and gradually wear away the top soft layer. As the water meets the board, it will fall over its edge and start to cut back in as it falls onto the softer rock below. As you keep pouring water, you should see your waterfall get bigger and a plunge pool start to develop. You may want to bail out some of the excess water at the bottom of the bowl from time to time, so your sand doesn't get washed away.

Erosion—Oceans and Ice

The power of the ocean waves and huge, moving slabs of ice can make dramatic changes to the landscape as they move rock from one place to another.

Shaping Our Coastlines

Waves crashing into ocean cliffs gradually wear away softer rock to form bays. The areas of harder rock left jutting out to sea are known as headlands.

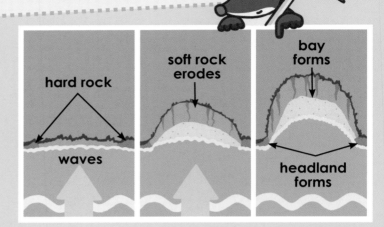

hard rock

soft rock erodes

waves

bay forms

headland forms

HANDS-ON Erode a Coastline

You will need:
• some sand
• some rocks
• a deep dish
• some water

Place a rock halfway down each side of the dish. Then form a straight coastline of sand between the two rocks. Pour water into the dish. Pat the water to create ocean waves. Watch your bay erode and your two headlands take shape.

Waves force their way into cracks in cliffs, bringing sand that grinds the rock to create caves. Spray pushes blowholes in cave roofs. Waves can wear right through headland to form an arch. Large arches collapse, leaving a column known as a stack. When a stack collapses, it forms a stump.

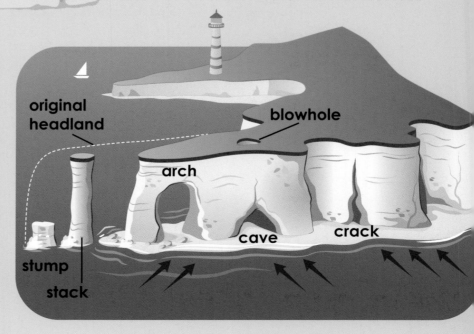

original headland

blowhole

arch

cave

crack

stump

stack

18

Enormous Moving Slabs of Ice

A **glacier** is a slow-moving river of ice that slides along Earth's surface. Glaciers can move huge boulders great distances and create vast, smooth, U-shaped valleys.

Glaciers move material in three ways.

- Meltwater freezes around cracked rock and then moves with the glacier, **plucking** the rock with it.

- Rock, frozen into the base of the glacier, scrapes the bedrock, and this abrasion moves other rock.

- Water in cracks in the bedrock freezes and thaws, eventually breaking off pieces of rock that move with the glacier.

plucking

abrasion

freeze-thaw

Think About This...

Which type of erosion do you think can move the largest rocks: Wind, water, or glacier?

BE A GEOLOGIST
How a Glacier Moves Boulders

You Will Need:

- a ziplock bag
- some water
- a freezer
- a tray of soil
- 2 or 3 small rocks
- a book

How to Do the Experiment:

Put the rocks into a ziplock bag and then fill the bag with water. Seal it and place it in the freezer overnight. Put a layer of soil in the tray. Prop up one end of the tray on a book to create a slope. Take your ice block out of the bag and place it at the top of the slope. Record where the rocks are deposited once the ice melts.

The Geology:

As the glacier melts, it will transport rock and soil down the slope with it.

Earth's Forces

Forces from deep inside Earth can cause weathering, and erosion too. Earth is made up of a series of **tectonic plates**, a little like a jigsaw. These plates move slightly as they float on the semiliquid layer beneath Earth's crust. When two plates stick and then suddenly release, this can cause an earthquake.

During an earthquake, rocks caught between moving plates may fracture into smaller fragments. Some underground fragments may make their way to the surface. The powerful shaking causes rocks on the surface to rub together. It can also cause **landslides**.

Think About This...

Do you know the name of the force that causes things to fall downward?

Landslides

Mudslides and landslides occur because of the pull of gravity on loose earth on a slope. Earthquakes, heavy rain, snow and ice, poor construction, and leaking underground pipes can all cause landslides. Rocks can be shattered into fragments as they fall down the slope. They will also rub against each other as they roll or slide.

HANDS-ON Earthquake!

You will need:
- a large book
- a rectangular cake pan
- four bouncy balls or marbles
- two large rubber bands
- two dry mud pies from page 9

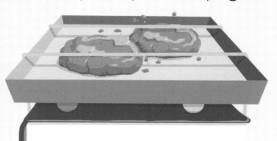

Experiment breaking up rock with earthquakes by making a shake table. Place four balls between a book and a cake pan. Wrap the rubber bands around the book and pan to hold everything in place. Wobbling the cake pan should make it shake as it rolls on the balls.

Put the mud pies in the pan and then shake it, like an earthquake. Do the mud pies start to weather? With how much force, and for how long, do you need to shake before they really start to break up?

BE A GEOLOGIST
How Does Rain Cause Landslides?

You Will Need:

- a plastic dish pan
- newspaper
- some mud
- spray bottle and water
- model houses
- small stones

How to Do the Experiment:

Fill one end of the dish pan with scrunched-up balls of newspaper. Press mud onto the newspaper to form a steep hillside. Place some model houses and stones on your slope. To create a landslide, spray water onto the hillside a little at a time.

How much water did it take before the mud started slipping down the hill? What happened to your model houses? Did your stones crash into each other?

The Geology:

Water adds weight to the slope and lowers the strength of the material so it is less able to withstand the force of gravity.

How Rivers Form a Valley

Most valleys and canyons are formed by rivers. The flowing water erodes the surrounding rock and wears it into sand and **silt**. River valleys are always changing as the river continually wears away the land through which they flow.

The river twists and turns around stones and other obstructions. Areas of slower and faster water movement cause the river to start to flow from side to side. The faster-moving water on the outside of a bend erodes more, and gradually forms a river cliff.

Rivers begin high up in the mountains. As they flow quickly downhill they cut a notch into the landscape. Rocks that fall into the fast-flowing river add to the erosion. The river becomes wider and deeper, creating a V-shaped valley.

Water moves slower on the inside of the bend. Deposited material often forms a beach. Erosion on the outer bank and deposits on the inner bank causes bends in the river known as **meanders**.

?

Not all valleys are formed by rivers. Glaciers and movement in Earth's plates can cause valleys to form too.

Oxbow lakes form from old bends in a river. When a river floods, the water sometimes finds a shorter route and goes across the bend rather than around it. The bend becomes a lake, separated from the river by deposited rock and silt.

Flooded areas can become very **fertile**. Sand, silt, minerals, and organic matter are brought to the areas when the river floods, which improves the soil.

HANDS-ON Make a River Valley

You will need:
- a tray of sand
- some small rocks
- a jug of water

Create a mountain landscape in a tray of sand. Slowly pour water from the jug over a mountain. Watch as your river valley forms, pulling sand and stones along with the flow of water.

How much force does your river need to move larger rock? Where does it deposit rock, and why? Move the rocks around. Does that alter the course of your river? Slow the flow of water. Can your river move rock now, or just sand?

Dangerous Erosion!

Erosion is a natural process, and it can be good for the environment. Erosion helps cleanse the soil of nutrient-poor dirt. It helps form incredible landscapes. But erosion can cause all kinds of problems too.

What's the Problem with Erosion?

- Eroded material can clog rivers and canals, causing flooding. Floods damage homes and farmland.

- Erosion can wash away good soil, making it impossible to grow crops. The world is losing soil faster than it can be formed again, which may mean we cannot grow enough food.

- Buried poisonous and plastic waste from old landfill sites can get exposed and washed into our oceans and rivers. Harmful fertilizers and other chemicals can get washed into low land, rivers, and oceans too.

- Erosion makes some land unstable. Whole villages have been lost over cliffs because of erosion. Large rockfalls, sinkholes, or landslides can bury roads or buildings.

- Rising sea levels and flooding due to climate change have increased soil and coastal erosion. If we tackle climate change, we will help slow dangerous erosion.

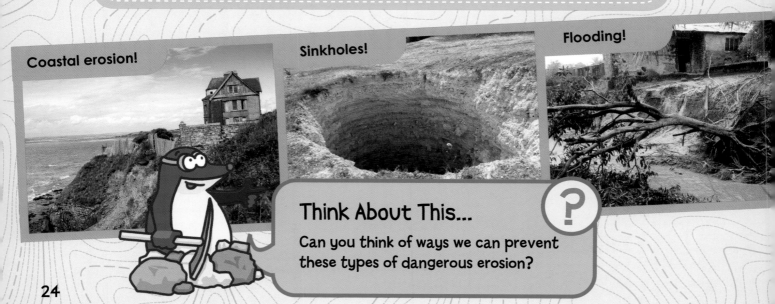

Coastal erosion!

Sinkholes!

Flooding!

Think About This...

Can you think of ways we can prevent these types of dangerous erosion?

How Do Sinkholes Happen?

Sinkholes occur when underground water dissolves soft rock such as salt and limestone. They develop underground for a long time before the hole appears. Water very slowly erodes the rocks and minerals. The surface above collapses, and a hole opens up. Drilling, mining, and broken water pipes can also cause sinkholes. Some sinkholes can be hundreds of miles (kms) wide and deep and swallow whole buildings!

BE A GEOLOGIST
Create a Sinkhole in a Paper Cup

You Will Need:

- sugar or flour
- sand or soil
- a toilet paper tube
- a plastic cup
- a small piece of sponge
- a bowl of water
- a tray

How to Do the Experiment:

Poke a hole in the bottom of a plastic cup. Put a piece of sponge in the cup, and place a toilet paper tube on the sponge. Place the cup on a tray to catch any spills. Pour sand or soil carefully around the tube. Then pour sugar or flour inside the tube.

Carefully remove the tube and you'll have a "soft rock" layer of sugar in the middle of your "hard rock" layer of sand. Cover the top with a little sand to represent the solid-looking ground over a sinkhole.

To mimic the underground water, get a jug of water. Hold the cup in the jug, just under the water level, so a little water starts to spill into the cup. Then quickly lift the cup back out. You should see a sink hole appear as the sugar dissolves.

The Geology:

In this experiment, the sugar represents easily eroded minerals. The sinkhole appears as the sugar is dissolved by the underground water quicker than the surrounding material is.

Slowing Erosion

We can't stop erosion, but we can slow it down. Along many coastlines, **climate change** is causing increased erosion. This means people living by the coast may lose their homes to the sea and we might lose important coastal environments like sand dunes.

Along the Coast

Breakwaters act as a wave barrier and protect boats.

Seawalls slow erosion, but are expensive and only protect the bit of coast they are built along.

Barriers jutting out to sea help trap sand on one side. They cause erosion on the other side, though, as waves hitting the shore at an angle cause sand to move in a zigzag pattern along the beach.

Plants' roots anchor the sand so it can't be blown or swept away.

Enlarging beaches by adding more sand can slow coastal erosion.

Fences act as windbreaks, keeping the wind from blowing sand away.

On the Land

Think About This...

How does covering the soil with plants, leaves, or matting help slow soil erosion?

Trees planted around farmland protect bare soil from the wind.

Moving grazing animals around helps grass grow back.

Slopes increase erosion, so flat terraces help keep soil from sliding away.

BE A GEOLOGIST
Test Which Materials Slow Soil Erosion

You Will Need:

adult help needed

- three cups
- some soil
- a tray
- a few books
- a small piece of turf
- some dead leaves
- three large plastic bottles
- an outdoor step
- a jug of water

The Geology:

Bare soil erodes quite easily. Adding a layer of leaves acts a little like an umbrella, protecting the soil from being washed away by rainfall. The grass protects the soil in the same way. The roots also help hold the soil in place and they soak up a lot of the water.

How to Do the Experiment:

Ask an adult to help you cut a large rectangle from the side of each of the plastic bottles. Do not cut off the neck or base. Place the bottles on their sides in a line on a tray, with the necks hanging over the edge. Put soil in two bottles. Put a layer of dead leaves on top of the soil in one bottle. Fill the last bottle with turf, along with its roots and soil. Put the tray on a step. Place a cup under each bottle's spout on the step below. If the bottles roll, wedge them with a few books.

Can you predict which bottle will erode the most soil? Make sure the cups are under the spouts. Carefully pour water into each bottle. You need to pour enough so water will come out of the bottletop, but not overflow the cups.

Examine the water in the cups. Which bottle eroded the most soil? Which cup has the cleanest water? Did that match your predictions?

Try propping the back of the tray on some books so the bottles form a slope. Does that change how much soil is eroded? Can you see why hill farmers make terraces?

Creating New Landforms

After material has been eroded, where does it go and what happens to it? Eroded material is eventually deposited by water, wind, or ice. As it settles, it can create new landforms. Landforms are natural features on the surface of Earth.

Wind deposits sand along this fence, creating a sand dune.

What causes material to be deposited?

Flowing water will eventually slow, or evaporate, winds die down, and glaciers melt. Anything that slows down water, or the force of the wind, will cause deposition. While erosion can destroy landscapes, deposition can create new ones.

Think About This...

Can you think of any landforms that are created by deposition?

HANDS-ON Explore Glacier Landforms

You will need:
- a paper cup
- dirt and gravel
- water
- a freezer
- 2 cups of flour
- cooking spray
- a baking sheet

Put a little dirt and gravel in a paper cup and then fill it to the top with water. Place it in a freezer overnight. Spray a baking sheet with cooking spray. Pour two cups of flour onto the tray and spread it out to make an even surface. Take your ice "glacier" out of the cup and place it at one end of the sheet. Press down and push the glacier across the sheet.

Examine the landforms it left in the flour. Glaciers create a valley, scraping the ground with rocks caught up in the ice. The mounds that form to the front and sides are known as **moraines**.

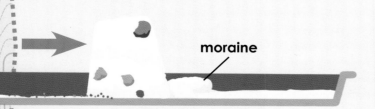

moraine

Sediment Forming Deltas

Rivers always flow toward a larger body of water. A delta is a wetland area that forms when a river slows as it empties into an ocean or lake. Sediment dropped at the mouth of the river builds up to form the delta. The river cuts small channels through the sediment.

BE A GEOLOGIST
Make a Delta Using a Stream Table

You Will Need:

adult help needed

- foil turkey pan
- scissors
- a bucket
- some books
- sand, small dead leaves and twigs, and gravel
- a small watering can
- a notebook and pencil
- a large trash bag

The Geology:

A river's shape changes depending on the type of soil and rock, the angle of the slope, and the amount of water. Try changing these things and see what happens. Where does your river landscape deposit sediment? Did you create a delta? Can you make your river alter its course?

How to Do the Experiment:

Cut a penny-size hole in the bottom of a turkey pan, near the edge of a short side. Mix 3 parts sand, 1 part dead leaves, and 1 part gravel. Put the mixture in the pan, opposite the hole, so it covers about two-thirds of the pan. Prop the soil end of the pan on some books. Hang the other end over the edge of a table. Cover the floor with the trash bag to catch any drips, and place a bucket under the hole.

Hold the watering can a ruler's height above the pan. Pour water onto the top of the slope. Make sure your bucket is catching the drips. A stream should start to form in the sand. In your notebook, draw and label any landforms that form.

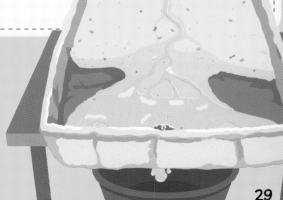

Glossary

abrasion a rubbing, grinding, or wearing away by friction.

acid rain rain with increased acidity caused by its environment.

bacteria single-celled microorganisms that live in soil, water, and the bodies of plants and animals.

biological weathering changes to exposed rocks, minerals, and soil caused by living things.

carbon dioxide a heavy colorless gas formed especially by the burning and breaking down of organic substances, and absorbed from the air by plants.

chemical weathering changes to exposed rocks, minerals, and soil caused by chemical reactions.

climate change a long-term change in the average weather patterns.

corrode to be eaten away by degrees.

current a body of water or air moving in a definite direction.

deposition the action or process of depositing.

deposits things laid or thrown down.

evaporates to pass off into vapor from a liquid state.

fertile producing vegetation or crops plentifully.

fossils traces, prints, or the remains of a plant or animal of a past age preserved in earth or rock.

fungi living things that lack chlorophyll, are parasitic or live on dead or decaying or,ganic matter.

glacier a large body of ice moving slowly down a slope or valley or spreading outward on a land surface.

gravity a force of attraction between particles or bodies that occurs because of their mass.

groundwater the water found underground in the cracks and spaces in soil, sand, and rock.

karst limestone landscape that has been eroded, producing ridges.

landscape the land that can be seen in one glance.

landslides the slippings of a mass of rocks or earth down a steep slope.

lichen plantlike living things made up of an alga and a fungus.

magma molten rock material inside Earth.

meanders turns or windings of a stream.

minerals solid chemical compounds that occur naturally in the form of crystals.

moraines piles of earth and stones carried and deposited by a glacier.

nitrogen a colorless, tasteless, odorless element that occurs as a gas. It makes up 78 percent of Earth's atmosphere and forms a part of all living tissues.

oxygen a colorless, tasteless, odorless gas that forms about 21 percent of Earth's atmosphere and is necessary for life.

particles very small parts of matter.

physical weathering changes to exposed rocks, minerals, and soil that affects their physical appearance.

plucking quickly removing something from its place.

sand dunes hills of sand near an ocean or in a desert formed by the wind.

sediment material such as stones and sand deposited by water, wind, or glaciers.

silt a soil made from very small particles of sediment from water.

sulfur a nonmetallic element.

tectonic plates large pieces of Earth's surface that move separately.

weathering the action of the forces of nature that change exposed rocks, minerals, and soil.

Further Information

Museums and Places to Visit

Visitors' centers. Your area may have caves, river canyons, wetlands, salt marshes ,or desert visitor centers where you could find information about erosion.

Local farms or farming museums. Farmers are very knowledgeable about the soil. There may be farms in your area that could show you how they help stop soil erosion.

Contact climate change action groups. Ask if you can join a local group that helps combat climate change.

Useful Websites

This Science for Kids Club website is packed with useful, easy-to-understand information about erosion.
https://www.scienceforkidsclub.com/erosion.html

A National Geographic webpage with information on erosion and links to related topics. It features clickable links to definitions of the terms used on the page.
https://www.nationalgeographic.org/encyclopedia/erosion/

A Learning Junction video cartoon with everything you need to know about soil erosion and how to prevent it.
https://www.youtube.com/watch?v=qNTOq1uEObc

Books to Read

Brannon, Cecelia H. *A Look at Erosion and Weathering (Rock Cycle)* New York, NY: Enslow Publishing, 2016.

Slipe, Nicole. *Restoring Muddy Creek (Smithsonian: Informational Text)*. Huntington Beach, CA: Teacher Created Materials, 2018.

Publisher's note to parents and teachers: Our editors have reviewed the websites listed here to make sure they're suitable for students. However, websites may change frequently. Please note that students should always be supervised when they access the internet.

Index